Unexpected:
Learning to love your unpredictable story

Brittany A. Meng

Unexpected: Learning to love your unpredictable story

© 2018 by Brittany A. Meng
ISBN: 9781717774811 KDP Independently published

THE HOLY BIBLE, NEW INTERNATIONAL VERSION®, NIV® Copyright © 1973, 1978, 1984, 2011 by Biblica, Inc.® Used by permission. All rights reserved worldwide.

Scripture taken from the New King James Version®. Copyright © 1982 by Thomas Nelson. Used by permission. All rights reserved.

Cover Design by Brittany A. Meng

Table of Contents

Unexpected

Brittany A. Meng

Welcome, friend

So, you're going through the unexpected right now, this very moment.

Maybe it's a diagnosis.

Maybe it's a move.

Maybe it's a broken bone or a broken heart; a lost job or a lost dream.

You're living with the uncertainty of the unexpected; perhaps you're dealing daily with unanswered questions, impatience, fear, anger, confusion, or hopelessness.

Maybe you want to move forward (in any way possible!)—physically, emotionally, or spiritually—but you just *can't.*

You feel stuck.

You're in the Waiting Place.

I've been there too. I could fill a bowl full of the Unexpected, a new flavor every other month.

From an unexpected twin pregnancy, to Autism and ADHD diagnoses for my kids, a miscarriage, the loss of my career, depression and anxiety, sudden moves, all the unpredictability that comes from being a military wife, and so much more.

I've been there too—in fact, as I write these words, I am still living in the crazy world of the unexpected.

My hope and prayer is that whether you are going through an unexpected season (or you love someone who is going through a hard time right now) my story will encourage you, give you new hope, and provide comfort and support as you bravely walk this unfamiliar path that God has placed before you.

1. It's okay not to be okay

"Are you okay?" My husband asked.

I almost said, "I'm fine" but I knew that was a lie (he knew it was too and would have called me out on it).

"No," I answered. "I'm not."

I was not fine. I was not okay.

As much as I wanted to be strong when my son was diagnosed with Autism...

As much as I wanted to rest in God's provision and peace when I lost our baby to miscarriage…

As much as I wanted to say "Thy will be done" when our dream overseas military assignment to England was unexpectedly jerked away from us…

I was not fine. I was not okay.

I was shocked by the unexpected, paralyzed when my plans fell apart, when the dream shifted, when the new path appeared with the road sign that said, "This way forward. You cannot go back."

But the longer I've had to sit with painful circumstances, the more I've come to realize this truth: *It's okay not to be okay.*

Somehow it is freeing for me to accept the fact that I am "not fine" right now.

When I started admitting the truth to myself, it also freed me to admit the truth to others too, like my husband, friends, and eventually, my counselor.

I started being more honest with God too. My prayers echoed David's honesty in Psalm 6: "Have mercy on me, O Lord, for I am weak…My soul also is greatly troubled" (Psalm 6:2-3 NKJV). It's comforting to know that I am not the only God-follower who has gone through agonizing circumstances.

Right now, you may be going through a painful, unexpected experience, or season, or year. It's okay to admit that what you are going through is hard.

It's okay not to be okay.

In Psalm 10:14 David also wrote this truth, "But you, God, see the trouble of the afflicted; you consider their grief and take it in hand" (NIV).

You may not be okay but hold on to this truth today: You are seen and you are loved, despite the unexpected journey you find yourself on.

God sees you. He sees your pain. He holds your grief in His hand.

Meditation Moment:
For I am convinced that neither death nor life, neither angels nor demons, neither the present nor the future, nor any powers, neither height nor depth, nor anything else in all creation, will be able to separate us from the love of God that is in Christ Jesus our Lord (Romans 8:38-39 NIV).

Are you being honest with yourself, others, and God about how you are doing right now? Tell God what is on your mind and in your heart. Ask Him to show you His love in a tangible way today.

2. When you can't embrace it

"You just have to embrace it."

I've heard these words so many times, most recently the "embrace the suck" tongue-in-cheek version of accepting the difficulties of military life.

Embrace it.

Wrap your arms around it.

Give it a squeeze.

Accept. Accept. Accept.

But what if you can't?

There are so many times in my life that I wanted, even *needed*, to jump in with both feet, when I needed to accept the unexpected:

When we learned that our son had a language processing learning disability that affected reading in the most challenging way

When I found myself as a SAHM when I longed for a career

When we had to move to a 900 square foot apartment with 4 kids and a dog after our military move plans fell through at the last minute (because we had already given up the lease on our house)

I longed to say, like my ever-patient, ever-practical husband, "It is what it is," shrug my shoulders and move on with life.

But I couldn't.

I felt like a 5-year-old at the family Christmas party who refused to join in the family picture.

"Uh huh."

"Nope."

"Don't wanna."

The frustratingly annoying part of acting like a 5-year-old when you are an adult is that you are fully aware of your own immaturity.

I knew I needed to accept these unexpected twists in our journey, but I couldn't make myself do it.

I needed time to get acquainted with the change.

I couldn't embrace it.

But I could shake hands.

I could shake hands, introduce myself, and simply sit beside the huge, life-altering reality that had just come into my life.

I could sit and wait, letting the unexpected soak in for a while.

"Embrace the change," they say.

Sometimes you can't, at least not right away.

But you can shake hands, acknowledge your reality and simply wait, giving yourself the grace you need to accept this new and unexpected journey.

Meditation Moment:
To everything there is a season,
A time for every purpose under heaven...
A time to weep,
And a time to laugh;
A time to mourn,
And a time to dance...
A time to embrace,
And a time to refrain from embracing;
A time to gain, and a time to lose;
A time to keep,
And a time to throw away...
He has made everything beautiful in its time
(Ecclesiastes 2:1;4; 5b-6; 11a NKJV).

Are you having a hard time embracing (or even shaking hands) with an unexpected situation? Spend some time reflecting about why it is hard to accept this situation right now. Give yourself permission, room, and space to embrace this change at your own pace.

3. Does it get easier?

For several years, I thought I had a good handle on my son's ADHD. Sure, we struggled but my tool bag of tips, tricks, and tried-and-true techniques kept us afloat.

But then we moved from Virginia to Texas. My son started struggling more. *We* started struggling more. My bag of tips, tricks, and techniques got a big hole in it and the bottom fell out of our mother-son relationship.

We needed help.

I heard this analogy once: Our burdens, both expected and unexpected, can be like holding a glass of water. It's easy to do for a little while. People tell you that you are so strong. They admire you (you admire yourself!). *I've got this,* you tell yourself.

But then, you have to hold the glass for an hour. Then six hours. Then a whole day. No switching hands, no breaks, no help.

Your arm would be screaming. Your hand would be shaking. You may even be crying from the exertion and pain of holding the glass of water all on your own.

The circumstance grows even more complex when our "glass of water" is a person that we love with all our hearts. It's our love that makes us strong, isn't it? It's love that helps us bear anything, do anything for the people we love.

But the longer you have to carry those burdens—searching for a job, chronic illness, a baby that doesn't sleep, special needs kids, aging parents, financial struggles, unfulfilled dreams, relationship struggles, whatever—the harder and more impossible the task seems.

The truth is, we get tired.

And then the situation shifts, ever so slightly, (like

our move) and the weight that we were used to carrying suddenly feels like it is about to crush us.

For me, coming to the end of myself and realizing that I couldn't cope with my own life—that I didn't know how to parent my son—was a pretty awful place to find myself.

It was also immensely freeing.

I sought out a counselor and after several months of sessions, where the counselor gave advice to both me and my son, our relationship got better.

My glass of water was too heavy for me to hold on my own. I was spilling out; I was breaking. I needed another hand to support me during that season.

I remember a dear friend telling me about the dark season she went through when she was caring for her dying mother: "I felt flat. I was so exhausted. I couldn't see the good in the world anymore."

She told me that she talked to her doctor and got a prescription for antidepressants.

"Did it help?" I asked.

"It did," she replied. "My mother passed away and I continued to take them for a little while longer. And then? I didn't need them anymore."

The medication was a hand on her glass of water during those difficult days.

Do burdens get easier to bear? Yes and no.

Yes, because we get stronger. Love makes us strong.

No, because we are human. We get tired physically, emotionally, mentally, and spiritually.

Asking for help doesn't mean you are weak. It means you've been strong for too long on your own. It's okay to admit to yourself and others that you need help carrying your burden. It's okay to reach out and ask for help. It's only then that we have the hope that things can get easier.

Meditation Moment:
When Moses' hands grew tired, they took a stone and put it under him and he sat on it. Aaron and Hur held his hands up—one on one side, one on the other—so that his hands remained steady till sunset (Exodus 17:12 NIV).

Is your glass of water getting too heavy for you to hold up on your own? Do you need help right now? Brainstorm ways you can get the support you need to help you walk though this season. Then take the first step: Make that phone call, send that email or text. Ask for help. It's okay.

4. Rooting out expectations

Before I had kids, I used to imagine what it would be like to be a mom. My daydreams were always filled with images of cooking, reading, laughing, and talking…to my daughters.

Having boys shocked me. Until my twins were about five, I was at a complete loss: *What do I do with these strange boy-creatures?*

I didn't know what they wanted, how their minds worked, or what their little bodies or hearts needed (turns out, mostly food, exercise, hugs, and someone listen to them talk about Star Wars).

When I had two *more* baby boys, I just threw up my hands and laughed. "Well, I know how this goes!"

I couldn't always laugh though. I went through some dark, confusing years as a young mom. I couldn't understand my children, what they needed, or how I, as their mother, could meet those needs. Their tiny male minds and bodies baffled me. Having boys was not what I expected. I had to come to grips with my expectations and let them go in order to fully love and enjoy the children that God gave me.

Other expectations have been harder to let go of, like expecting school to come easily for our kids. My husband was identified as gifted as a child. School was always easy for him–in fact, he was bored through most of his formal schooling. He never had to study. In high school, he slept through an entire semester of biology and still got a four out of five on the AP Biology Exam. He expected that his sons would follow in his footsteps (not in the sleeping, just the ease).

However, after several years of struggling in school, our son was identified with a language processing learning disability, which greatly affects reading and listening. He also struggles with fine motor skills, like handwriting.

Identifying his learning disabilities was a huge process, but relatively straight forward.

Identifying our expectations, which manifested themselves in frustration and even disappointment, was much more difficult.

It's incredibly painful to look your expectations in the face, to acknowledge that they do not match your reality, to swallow your pride, to cast aside those expectations, and then embrace (or just shake hands?) your life the way it truly is.

We have struggled: Struggled with our disappointments, and then our guilt at being disappointed; we've struggled to understand, accept, and even love the child we have.

We've struggled with the dark truth in our own hearts and the grief that permeates the whole situation. And that grief is painful. But it's pride that's wounded, the clinging to self-important dreams of what we thought our life "should" look like.

But before we could accept the gifts we had been given, our expectations had to be rooted out of our hearts so we could accept the path that was now before us.

This path.

This way.

This child.

Yes, Lord. This child.

What a gift.

Meditation Moment:

Let us throw off everything that hinders and the sin that so easily entangles. And let us run with perseverance the race marked out for us, fixing our eyes on Jesus, the pioneer and perfecter of faith. For the joy set before him he endured the cross, scorning its shame, and sat down at the right hand of the throne of God (Hebrews 12: 1b-2 NIV).

Are you dealing with disappointment and frustration in your current situation? How did you expect things to go? Give yourself permission to honestly acknowledge your expectations and begin the grieving process of letting those expectations go.

5. Don't miss the mark

So often, especially lately, I feel so angry at situations that are outside of my control.

When I struggle to communicate and relate to my older sons specifically because of issues related to their ADHD.

When I'm faced (again) with the impossibly slow and ever-changing military schedule.

When I, once more, have to address my own immaturity and negative emotional responses that rise up when my life feels out of control.

These words turn round and round in my mind as I struggle: "In your anger, do not sin" (Ephesians 4:26 NIV). This is a challenging verse for me because so often, the anger itself seems wrong. I want to get rid of my "bad" feelings. I hate feeling helpless, out of control, and then reacting in rage. I just want to not feel. So, I push my anger down, willing myself to be "fine. Yes, I'm fine. I don't want to talk about it."

After all, this out of control situation is in God's hands, right? He's in control, so I need to be fine with it. But I've found that when I push my anger down, it tends to come out sideways, like when I lash out at my husband because our moving plans have been postponed…again (It's not his fault. He's doing all he can to move the process along).

Recently, I watched a video on the word "sin" presented by *The Bible Project* (available on YouTube). The root meaning of the word is "to miss the mark," like an archer who may hit the target but miss the bullseye (or fail to hit the target all together!).

When I insert this phrase in Ephesians 4:26, it has helped me address my anger in a new light: "In your anger, do not miss the mark."

My anger, when it rises within me, simply *is*—it's a neutral, though powerful, emotion. It's what I do with my anger that determines whether or not I "miss the mark."

Lately, I've been trying to name my emotions for what they are: Not "frustrated," not "annoyed," not "upset": I AM ANGRY. I've also been trying to identify who or what I am really angry at: is it really my spouse, or my kids, or the military?

If I'm painfully honest with myself, I'm often angry at God.

For some reason, that's a hard truth to swallow. As Jesus followers, we aren't supposed to get angry with God. But if we read the Bible, we can see that we aren't the only ones.

David wrote, "How long, Lord? Will you forget me forever? How long will you hide your face from me?" (Psalm 13: 1 NIV).

Asaph, a Psalm-writer, lamented, "We are given no signs from God; no prophets are left, and none of us knows how long this will be" (Psalm 74:9 NIV).

Even Job, who did not sin against God by voicing his anger at his situation, stated, "I cry out to you, God, but you do not answer; I stand up, but you merely look at me" (Job 30:20 NIV).

I once confessed to a friend that I was angry with God, and she told me, "Tell Him about your feelings. He can handle it."

And so, I'm learning.

I'm learning to be honest with myself and honest with God. I'm also learning about my own motivations for telling God about my anger, realizing that it isn't so much about receiving answers, but knowing that I am heard.

I also realize that my anger can drive a wedge between myself and God, just like it can in my human relationships. When I see that my anger is causing a breakdown in relationship—like when I don't want to pray or I feel perpetually cynical about my spiritual life—I know that I have missed the mark.

Getting angry about situations that are outside of my control is part of the reality of what it means to be human in a fallen world. Accepting this truth, identifying my anger, honestly dialoging about how I feel with God and others, and continuing to seek relationship even in the middle of difficult emotional situations, is helping me to be angry yet not miss the mark, and to continue to seek maturity in this difficult area of my life.

Meditation Moment:
How long, Lord? Will you forget me forever?
   How long will you hide your face from me?
How long must I wrestle with my thoughts
   and day after day have sorrow in my heart?
   How long will my enemy triumph over me?

Look on me and answer, Lord my God.
   Give light to my eyes, or I will sleep in death,
and my enemy will say, "I have overcome him,"
   and my foes will rejoice when I fall.

But I trust in your unfailing love;
   my heart rejoices in your salvation.
I will sing the Lord's praise,
   for he has been good to me (Psalm 13 NIV).

Are you "missing the mark" with you anger? Think and pray about how you can be honest about your feelings without pushing them down or damaging your relationships. If needed, seek restoration in a relationship that has been damaged by your anger.

6. What you meant for evil

I felt paralyzed when she told me.

"You were raped?" I repeated, wishing it was just a nightmare.

But it wasn't even my nightmare. I was on the outside looking in, doing all I could to comfort, encourage, and advocate but knowing in my heart that nothing I did would erase the injustice and agony executed on my dear friend.

In the weeks and months to come, I found myself swallowing back my words as I searched for ways to comfort her.

How could I tell her "all things work together for good to those who love God" (Romans 8:28 NKJV)?

How could I tell her "Jesus is with you—He will never leave you or forsake you"?

Where was He that night?!

How could God let this happen to her?!

Even now, years later, the tears rise as I remember the fury and helplessness I felt as I watched this beautiful young woman fold in upon herself as the semester continued, her weight and grades dropping, the shadows beneath her eyes deepening. She couldn't sleep. Nightmares tormented her every time she closed her eyes.

My fury increased, especially after the university administration said it was a case of "he said, she said" after she bravely went forward to tell her story.

Why? *Why*? WHY?!

As I wrestled with my anger and grief, I cried out to God. But my prayers were not ones of acceptance or "Thy will be done."

They were crammed with anguished questions, rage-filled accusations, and bitter tears.

From David to Job to Hannah to Jeremiah, the Old Testament is filled with the stories and laments of people who have cried out to God in their anguish, demanding answers and justice.

In those months, when I cried out to God on behalf of my dear friend, I didn't receive answers and she didn't receive justice.

But He did remind me of a story that helped to bring a longed-for stillness to the emotional hurricane in my soul.

He reminded me of the story of Joseph; he had been sold into slavery by his own brothers, then unjustly accused and imprisoned; he rose to be second-in-command in Egypt and saved his family and the nations from starvation. After all that pain, Joseph was able to see God's thread of providence woven throughout his life.

"'But as for you,' he told his brothers, 'you meant evil against me; but God meant it for good, in order to bring it about as it is this day, to save many people alive'" (Genesis 50:20 NKJV).

After God brought this story to my mind, I knew I had a choice to make: I could choose to cling to my anger and bitterness (which I knew in my heart were not serving me or my friend) or I could choose, by faith, to trust that God can take the evil done against us and those we love and use it for His glory and good.

Slowly, tentatively, I released my anger and bitterness and chose to trust God, even though to this day, I feel the emotional weight of this horrible, unexpected, wicked circumstance.

The semester after her rape, my friend moved away and went through some very dark years. But, as I have followed her life from afar on social media, I've seen beautiful evidence of God's grace and healing. She is now married to a wonderful, caring man, works in a high school ministry, and is training to become a foster parent.

I never shared Joseph's story with her.

It wasn't the right time all those years ago; some things, even though they are true, do not bring comfort in the moment. Instead, I tried to do my best to love her and listen in the difficult aftermath.

The truth God revealed to me during that hard season was for me. I needed to learn to trust Him in a deeper way, to realize that even in situations of great evil, He is still the God who sees.

He knows our pain; He collects our tears; He is not blind to injustice.

He holds our lives in His hand and He can bring goodness and light into the darkest, most unexpected places, even if in the moment, the light is only a flicker in the distance.

Meditation Moment:
I will lead the blind by ways they have not known,
    along unfamiliar paths I will guide them;
I will turn the darkness into light before them
    and make the rough places smooth.
These are the things I will do;
    I will not forsake them (Isaiah 42:16 NIV).

Is someone you love suffering? Pray for this person now. Ask God to help you know how to comfort this person. If you are experiencing anger and grief as the result of injustice done to a person that you love, ask God to help you to work through these emotions.

7. Was it my fault?

"Hey, listen to this…" My husband said one night as we sat together on the couch after the kids were (blessedly) in bed. He launched into a brief description of an article he was reading about the effects of breastmilk on newborn brain development.

He knew that I loved articles like that. But on this day, as soon as he stopped talking, I burst into tears.

"Do you think that's maybe why the boys have the challenges they do? Because they had to go to the NICU when they were born? Because I couldn't breastfeed them right away? What if it's all my fault?" I cried. "What if—"

"Brittany." He cut me off, firmly but tenderly. "It is not your fault. Look at me."

I did, tears rolling down my cheeks, my aching heart spilling out all its hoarded doubts.

"It is *not* your fault."

He then went on to recite all the prenatal care I received during my twin pregnancy, all the specialists we saw, all the vitamins I took, all the "Nutrition by Trimester" books and articles I read, all the injections, non-stress tests, and ultrasounds I received to make sure my boys were living and growing.

I listened, willing my heart to believe him but, like a bad habit, my mind jumped to self-damning questions: *What if it was all the ultrasounds? Did I do something to cause my sons' learning disabilities, ADHD, sensory processing issues, and developmental challenges?*

It's human nature to ask "Why" when the unexpected happens. Then, when we dig a little deeper, into the dark corners of our hearts, the question becomes, *Is it my fault? Is it something I did?*

So often, when we question the unexpected events of our lives—the ones not caused by our mistakes or our sin—we rarely receive the answers to these questions on this side of heaven (and maybe not on the other side either—the Bible isn't really clear on that).

Jesus, though, offers us a new perspective. In the story about the man born blind, Jesus' disciples ask, "Rabbi, who sinned, this man or his parents, that he was born blind?"

And Jesus said, "Neither this man nor his parents sinned, but this happened so that the works of God might be displayed in him" (John 9:1-3 NIV).

Then Jesus heals the man, giving sight to his blind eyes.

While initially, the man seems elated and becomes Jesus' disciple, I've often wondered if, later, the man was confused, even angry—"I had to suffer my entire life *just* so God could get the glory?!"

The man didn't cause his blindness; his parents didn't cause his blindness. Yet, as a result, this person—as a baby, a young boy, as man—suffered. His mother and father suffered. His whole family suffered.

Did they ask, *Why? Why, God? Why did this happen? Was it something we did?*

I'm sure they did. They were human, after all, just like us.

When Jesus healed this man, He first spat in the dirt, made mud, spread it over the man's eyes, and told him to go wash in the pool of Siloam. The man did as Jesus said and his eyes were opened.

The man did as Jesus said and his eyes were opened.

Could we, perhaps, receive a new perspective on our unexpected sufferings if we do as Jesus says?

If we seek to love God and love others, to pursue the presence and likeness of Christ in our hardships, in the times when we have no answers, will our eyes, too, be opened?

I don't think our hearts will ever stop longing for answers, but in the midst of our trials, may we surrender to His way, waiting for the day when our doubts will be replaced with truth, believing that, if we are open and ready, the works of God will be displayed in us, rising from the ashes of our deepest suffering.

Meditation Moment:
"I, the Lord, have called You in righteousness,
And will hold Your hand;
I will keep You and give You as a covenant to the people,
As a light to the Gentiles,
To open blind eyes,
To bring out prisoners from the prison,
Those who sit in darkness from the prison house.
I am the Lord, that is My name;
And My glory I will not give to another,
Nor My praise to carved images.
Behold, the former things have come to pass,
And new things I declare;
Before they spring forth I tell you of them" (Isaiah 42:6-9 NIV).

Do you beat yourself up with unanswerable questions, wondering if "it is all your fault?" Ask God to give you a new perspective today, to open your eyes to see how this current suffering or unexpected circumstance can be used to display His works in your life or in the lives of others.

8. Anxiety and peace

I've struggled with anxiety since I was a young girl on the brink of puberty.

And when I say "anxiety," I mean the chemical kind, like when your hormones are messed up, your fight-or-flight is on full-throttle, and at times you need medication to help you function like a "normal" human being (Thank God for medication. It has helped me through some difficult seasons of life). This is physical/chemical anxiety.

However, as I read my Bible as a young girl and woman, I thought that the constant knot in the pit of my stomach and racing thoughts I experienced were a spiritual failing on my part.

I memorized this scripture, desperately praying over and over again, "Be anxious for nothing, but in everything by prayer and supplication, with thanksgiving, let your requests be made known to God; and the peace of God, which surpasses all understanding, will guard your hearts and minds through Christ Jesus" (Philippians 4: 6-7 NIV).

And I waited for the peace to come, the calm that I longed for to wash over my fluttering heart, to untangle my knotted gut.

But it didn't.

Not because I wasn't praying the right prayers, or supplicating hard enough, or wasn't thankful, or didn't believe. No, the peace I longed for wasn't present because I didn't understand my own chemical make-up or how to make my body and mind work in a whole and healthy way. I was also using God like a vending machine: I give You prayers and thanksgiving; You make me feel peaceful.

But primarily, I had a foundational misunderstanding

of both "anxiety" and "peace."

While at times in my life, I had little understanding and control over my physical/chemical anxiety, I am often a willing participant in spiritual/emotional anxiety.

Spiritual/emotional anxiety is worry in action, the frantic circling back over worn out paths of unanswerable questions and what-ifs, obsessively focusing on problems that I cannot solve, forgetting to remember that God is God and I am not.

Prayer and thanksgiving are spiritual medicine for this type of anxiety, especially prayers that remind me to focus firmly on today and not to speculate about tomorrow, reminding me that I am a created being and not the orchestrator of the universe, my own or anyone else's (thank God for that).

But more recently, coming to a more comprehensive understanding of "peace" has helped me have a more healing and holistic view of how to address my every day anxieties in a way that honors God.

The biblical word for "peace" in Hebrew is "Shalom" and in Greek it is "Eirene." The most basic meaning of "Shalom" is "complete" or "whole," like a wall encircling a city that has "no gaps or missing bricks. Shalom refers to something that is complex with lots of pieces that is in a state of completeness.

"The core idea is that life is complex, with lots of moving parts and relationships and situations and when any of these is out of alignment or missing, your shalom breaks down.

"To bring shalom literally means to 'make complete' or 'restore'…True peace requires taking what is broken and restoring it to wholeness, whether it is in our lives, our relationships, or in our world" (Jon Collins and Time Mackie, *The Bible Project*, "Peace", YouTube.com).

With this comprehensive definition in mind, I have been able to develop a more complete understanding of what God promises in Philippians 4. He isn't promising "emotional calm" or the absence of stress; rather, Paul states that God's "wholeness," His completeness will fill in the gaps of our anxious uncertainty when our personal shalom breaks down.

Worrying over the future or those unexpected circumstances we cannot control does not bring about the holiness that God wants to create in us today.

Yet when we come to Him with our worries, telling Him all that is in our hearts, practicing thankfulness in the middle of uncertainty, God's peace, like a strong, perfect wall surrounding a city, will encircle our hearts and minds as we press forward in pursuing Christ Jesus.

May we all have more complete view of His peace in our lives today.

And may we strive to be peace makers in our own lives, encircling others with love, and filling in the gaps when the shalom breaks down around us.

Meditation Moment:
The Lord is my rock and my fortress and my deliverer;
My God, my strength, in whom I will trust;
My shield and the horn of my salvation, my stronghold
(Psalm 18:2 NKJV).

Blessed are the peacemakers,
For they shall be called sons of God (Matthew 5:9
NKJV).

Are you experiencing anxiety? What kind of anxiety is it: physically/chemical, emotional/spiritual? Both?
Consider the ways you can address your anxiety in a restorative, wholistic way in order to bring about shalom in your life.
Ask God to surround you with His peace, filling in the

gaps of uncertainty in your life.

9. Transitions

"I don't think I do transitions very well," I told my counselor. "How do I go through this military transition gracefully?"

After eleven years of marriage, I stopped saying "no" to my husband's desire to become a military officer and we were about to leap into a completely new life. Yet, even after I talked through my fears, expectations, and thought-patterns with my counselor about my future, I still don't have a clear, put-your-finger-on-it answer.

How do you go through transitions gracefully? I asked myself. *How do you accept change—even good change—when the world you are stepping into is completely unknown?*

I thought of other transitions I've gone through, some that nearly did me in, like becoming a mom to twin boys at age twenty-three; getting an Autism diagnosis for our son when he was eight; struggling with breastfeeding my fourth son; and quitting my job after I worked so hard in grad school to become a University English instructor.

But this military transition has been one of the most challenging. My husband jokes that we aren't starting a new chapter in our lives—we're starting a new volume.

Somehow, though, it's a small comfort to know that transitions are part of what it means to be human. The only constant is change, right?

There's transition in starting—and ending a job.

There's pain in the transformation of becoming a parent for the first time, and pain and adjustment in an empty nest.

There are health transitions and wealth transitions.

There's death—of loved ones, pets, relationships, and dreams.

I've done more stumbling than waltzing through my life transitions, fumbling in the dark for something called "Normal."

And I think that's where I've missed the mark—I've been searching for "Normal."

When I had my twins, the life I knew dissolved before my eyes. I spent weeks, months, trying to cling to my pre-kids life, my past identity, my marriage, friendships, body image, time management, hobbies, sleep, the life-as-I-knew-it-before-kids.

But the thing is, my pre-kids life was gone. *Poof!* It was no more. And the harder I tried to get back to that place, that Old Normal, the more frustrated, confused, and discontent I became about my new life.

I couldn't go back. I could only move forward.

There's grief in the moving forward, in the unclenching of fingers from dreams and memories that are already slipping away.

There's grief in the letting go. It's hard to say goodbye, especially to a life well-lived, to a season of satisfaction, to the familiar, to whatever feels like home.

I don't know what the future holds, but as I go through this transition, I'm clinging to faith that God still has so much Good in store for me in the future, despite all the unknowns.

Embracing the grief.

Believing in the Good.

Moving forward.

Maybe those are the keys to graceful transition.

Meditation Moment:
When you pass through the waters,
    I will be with you;
and when you pass through the rivers,
    they will not sweep over you…

Forget the former things;
 do not dwell on the past.
See, I am doing a new thing!
 Now it springs up; do you not perceive it?
I am making a way in the wilderness
 and streams in the wasteland (Isaiah 43: 2a;18-19 NIV).

Are you going through a time of transition right now? Write down three things that you are grieving over. Take some time to be sad.
Write down three things that you are looking forward to in the future. Ask God to help you anticipate to the good things He has planned for you.

10. God's goodness

Twenty minutes after I received the phone call, we got the expected knock at the front door. A friend from church was bringing us dinner.

I was still numb from the news: "Your numbers are dropping. I'm afraid this confirms a miscarriage."

As our friend set the food on the table, we told her what happened. She was so sorry. She had been praying for us fervently. She even shared that she had seen a vision of God cradling my womb during her prayers.

"Can I pray for you now?" she asked. She slipped her arm around me in our kitchen and we bowed our heads. "Oh, Lord," she began. "We thank you for your goodness…"

Everything in me recoiled. How could she *thank God for His goodness*? This was not good! This was bad, horrible, a nightmare! If God was good, then why did my baby die? I begged God to let the baby live, let the bleeding stop, let the midwife say "We have good news!"

That was the phone call I played over and over again in my mind. I didn't even mentally entertain the alternative. The pain was beyond my imagination.

Yet here I was, in the midst of it.

And she was thanking God for His goodness?!

God was not good. Not to me.

Her prayer and God's presence hovered over my soul at that moment and I shoved them away as hard as I could.

I couldn't pray. I had no words, only deep pain and suffering that I had never experienced before. Oh, I had suffered, of course, but as a result of my sin, or someone else's. That suffering had a reason, a purifying effect, a course that led me to repentance.

But this? This was new. Stark and bleak, shocking, numbing and white hot. Suffering that assaulted me physically, emotionally, and spiritually.

"We know you are a good God…" she prayed.

I wanted to laugh. But I couldn't, so I cried.

We know you are a good God.

I don't remember anything else from her prayer in my kitchen that day. But her words about God's goodness both shocked me and have stuck with me.

We *know* you are a good God.

I knew, in my head, that God is good. I had repeated those words since I was a child. I had memorized hundreds of verses, could recite every Bible story that spoke to this truth. I had prayed these words myself.

I had never doubted God's goodness.

Until now.

I doubted in my heart because it was filled with so much pain that there wasn't room for my faith.

I heard a song a few days later, a familiar hymn: "His eye is on the sparrow, and I know He watches me." I basked in the comfort of the verse that inspired this song ("Are not two sparrows sold for a penny? Yet not one of them will fall to the ground outside your Father's care" Matthew 10:29 NIV) but a moment later was slammed with this truth: *His eye is on the sparrow…but the sparrow still falls.*

And all I can ask is why? Why did He let the sparrow fall? That was my only prayer:

Why did this happen, God?

I don't know why. But I do know He is with me, watching me. And weeping with me.
This is faith. Horrible, hard, gut-wrenching faith: the truth that God is good.

Meditation Moment:

The Lord is good,
   a refuge in times of trouble.
He cares for those who trust in him (Nahum 1:7 NIV).

The Lord is close to the brokenhearted
   and saves those who are crushed in spirit (Psalm 34:18
NIV).

*How has God been good to you? If you are having
trouble trusting that He is good right now, reflect on
how He has been good to you in the past.
If that is difficult too, think about how He brought His
people through difficult situations in the Bible.
Ask Him to help you see His goodness to you in new,
surprising, and comforting ways.*

11. Thankful in

I shuffled into the kitchen, pushing the Keurig button and shoving my greasy hair behind my ear. I was awake. I was functioning. I could make eggs. I could feed my kids breakfast before school…

…before I went to lay on the couch for the rest of the day.

It was a few days since "the phone call" and I was in the "wait and see" days of what they call "miscarriage management."

My son Micah pushed play on our kitchen CD player and Psalty the Singing Songbook's perky voice filled the air: "In everything give thanks! In every situation! Sing of song of thanks…and praise Him from your heart!!!"

This is such a stupid song, I thought. *There is nothing, NOTHING to be thankful for in this situation. Everything about this sucks. Miscarriage SUCKS!*

I put plastic plates of eggs in front of my kids and sat down heavily at the table in our eat-in kitchen, wincing from pain in my womb and pain in my heart. Then I glanced over at my toddler, Silas, sitting in his highchair. He smiled at me.

Precious little boy. You are such a comfort to me.

I pushed through the fog in my brain and tried to plan my day…dinner tonight? Oh! That's right. Another dear friend was bringing us a meal.

I'm so glad I don't have to cook tonight. Thank you, Lord, for friends and the meal.

Aaron came into the kitchen and kissed me on the forehead. "Ready to go to school, boys?"

Thank you for my husband. He has taken such good care of me and the kids.

"Bye, Mommy!" My twins said as four skinny arms encircled my waist. "See you after school!"

Thank you for my children.
I have three beautiful children who love me.
I am blessed. I am *blessed.*

The realization washed over me: "*In* everything give thanks…."

Not *for* everything.

In this moment, this deep, difficult season, I couldn't be thankful *for*…but I could be thankful *in*.

I *needed* to be thankful…because thankfulness is ultimately trust in God.

My brief prayers of thanks that morning revealed that God was still taking care of me. He holds my whole life in His hands, both the good and the bad. Thankfulness is recognizing this truth.

Despite the pain, despite the heartache, despite the unexpected, give thanks in all things.

This is the will of God for you.

Meditation Moment:
Rejoice always, pray continually, give thanks in all circumstances; for this is God's will for you in Christ Jesus…May God himself, the God of peace, sanctify you through and through. May your whole spirit, soul and body be kept blameless at the coming of our Lord Jesus Christ. The one who calls you is faithful, and he will do it (1 Thessalonians 5: 16-18; 23-24 NIV).

What can you be thankful IN today? Take a few moments and write a list of all you have to be thankful for today, even in this season of uncertainty.

12. Walking through the valley

When I first learned that I had miscarried, I felt numb. I remember laying on my bed and trying to pray. But I had no words.

Psalm 23:4 came to my mind: "Yea though I walk through the Valley of the Shadow of Death, I will fear no evil, for You are with me…" (NKJV).

In my mind's eye, I saw this Valley—razor sharp mountains, void of any vegetation, pierced the sky. The Valley was dusky, dark and grey. The path jutted sharply into shadows; I couldn't see beyond a few steps. I was afraid, horrifically afraid…because I knew the way was full of pain, deep physical and emotional pain.

I DON'T WANT THIS PATH! I DIDN'T CHOOSE THIS PATH! My mind screamed. I mentally dug in my heels. I wouldn't go. I would not walk this path. I refused.

But there wasn't another way.

This was The. Only. Way.

…I will fear no evil, for You are with me.

Brittany, He whispered to my soul. *I am already there, in the Valley.*

But this did not comfort me. The Valley was a dark, painful place; God's presence could not change that. All I could think was if God is already there, I didn't want to follow. But there was no going back. The only way was through the Valley.

I prayed, *Please be with me. Please be with me. Pleasebewithme…*

I felt utterly alone. My pain was bound up in my body, without any cathartic release. I couldn't give it away if I wanted to. No one could carry this burden with me. No one understood.

Even though I walk through the Valley of the Shadow

of Death...You are with me...

As I walked through the seemingly endless days of grief, the verse became a mantra, playing over and over again in my mind.

At times it comforted me.

Other times, it frustrated me.

But after one extremely difficult day in the weeks following the miscarriage, I saw this verse in a new light.

God wasn't just with me, beside me. He promised that his Spirit was within me, inside my soul—inside my body, my body that was filled with so much physical and emotional anguish.

He was inside me—feeling, suffering, mourning, grieving, *with me.*

I used to think that when God walked with a person through hard times, the darkness of that person's path would somehow be filled with His light.

My path through the valley was not filled with light. And yet, years later, when I think about those dark days, I remember the darkness, but I also remember His presence.

Even through the Valley of the Shadow of Death, He *was* with me.

Meditation Moment:
The Lord is my shepherd;
I shall not want.
He makes me to lie down in green pastures;
He leads me beside the still waters.
He restores my soul;
He leads me in the paths of righteousness
For His name's sake.
Yea, though I walk through the valley of the shadow of death,
I will fear no evil;

For You are with me;
Your rod and Your staff, they comfort me.
You prepare a table before me in the presence of my
enemies;
You anoint my head with oil;
My cup runs over.
Surely goodness and mercy shall follow me
All the days of my life;
And I will dwell in the house of the Lord
Forever (Psalm 23, NKJV).

*Are you walking through the Valley of the Shadow of
Death today? Are you grieving deeply? Pray Psalm 23
over your life and ask God to help you feel His presence
and faithfulness with you today.*

13. Singing with doubt

I wish I could say that my prayers during difficult seasons have been, "Teach me your ways, Oh Lord." But they've been more desperate, something more like, "Help me, *please*."

And He has helped me: through therapy, counseling, books, support and understanding from family and friends, and by giving me hope for the future.

God has cared for me like a good, good Father.

We sing "Good, Good Father" at church (Pat Barrett and Tony Brown). I really enjoy this song. It's comforting, especially during times of uncertainty and hardship. But the song has also exposed my lack of faith and the holes in my professed acceptance of my boys' special needs.

The bridge of the song refers to God being perfect in every way, in all of His planning and purpose for our lives. There have been Sundays where those words have had such a bad taste that I wanted to spit them out of my mouth. It's one thing to accept that special needs like learning disabilities and ADHD are a fixed part of our family life. It's another thing to declare that this was part of God's perfect plan.

Really, God?! With this, too?

After all, the neurological differences my sons face are imperfections. They make life difficult, challenging, and even heart-breaking at times for our family.

And I ask, disdainfully, *How can this be part of Your "perfect plan"?*

But in my bitter, soul-questioning of God's sovereignty, my prayers have shifted. *Teach me.*

It's a prayer that exposes my doubt because the unstated confession is this: *Teach me...because I don't believe in your perfect plan.*

I used to think that parents of special needs kids have some sort of divine favor or anointing from God, some sort of extra grace. I can't speak for everyone but it's far from true for me.

This isn't the parenting story I would have written for myself. But God gave me my boys and said, "Parent them. Raise them. Love them. I will never leave you or forsake you."

So, I pray, "Help my unbelief," like the desperate father crying out to Jesus for stronger faith (Mark 9:24). I wish I could tell you that I'm at home in the reality of my own life, that I can say "Thank you" in full acceptance for what I've been given.

But many times, I can't.

I do know that soul-wrestling has made me stronger and praying *Teach Me* along with *Help Me* has gotten easier lately.

Maybe that means that my faith is getting stronger too.

And when I sing about God's perfect sovereignty over my life, it's an act of faith, because singing with doubt is better than not singing at all.

Meditation Moment:
Because of the Lord's great love we are not consumed,
    for his compassions never fail.
They are new every morning;
    great is your faithfulness.
I say to myself, "The Lord is my portion;
    therefore I will wait for him."
The Lord is good to those whose hope is in him,
    to the one who seeks him;
it is good to wait quietly
    for the salvation of the Lord (Lamentations 3:22-26 NKJV).

When you look at the unexpected circumstances of your life, do you question God's "perfect ways"? Spend some time thinking about your doubts and honestly talk to God about them. Ask Him to "help your unbelief."

14. Comfort

My little boy was crying, sobbing really, and I had no idea why.

I stepped into his dark room, rushed over to his crib, and lifted his chubby toddler body into my arms.

"Lay your head, baby," I murmured, placing a gentle hand on his downy hair as I settled into the rocking chair.

As he continued to sob, I found myself wishing, like I always did in these middle-of-the-night-moments, that I still had milk to soothe him, but I had weaned him a month before his second birthday. Instead, I stroked his hair and his cheeks, wiping the tears away.

At his tender age, he had no words to describe what was wrong.

A bad dream?

A tummy ache?

I had no idea. So, I just told him, "Mama's here. Mama's here. Shhhh…Mama's here, sweetheart."

We rocked and rocked. Gradually his cries turned to whimpers and then, slowly, his shuddering sighs became deep, even breaths.

Is he asleep? I shifted to catch a glimpse of his face in the soft glow of the hall light that was streaming into his room, but the tightening grip of his soft, plump arms around my neck told me he was not.

He needed me. He couldn't tell me about his pain, whether it was emotional or physical, but I was here for however long he needed.

So, we rocked and rocked.

I rubbed his back and kissed his sweet, soft head over and over again.

"I love you," I whispered. "I love you."

A little while later, when I laid my heavy, drowsy baby in bed, I was struck by the holiness of this mundane moment, this middle of the night meeting between mother and child: *This is how God wants to comfort us.*

He is there when we cry out in the night with our physical, emotional, spiritual pain. Like a loving mother, He longs to take us in His arms and wipe our tears, to comfort us in our fears, to be with us in those aching, impossible moments that have no words and no easy answers.

Wherever you are today on this unexpected journey, if you are crying out to God in your heart and soul for comfort, I pray that in your holy imagination you will experience the comfort of His love in a deep, tangible way, like a mother soothing her child in the darkness of the night.

Lay your head, my darling.
I am here.
I am here.
I love you.

Meditation Moment:
As a mother comforts her child,
    so will I comfort you;
    and you will be comforted over Jerusalem (Isaiah 66:13 NIV).

But I have calmed and quieted myself,
    I am like a weaned child with its mother;
    like a weaned child I am content.
Israel, put your hope in the Lord
    both now and forevermore (Psalm 131:2-3 NIV).

Are you or is someone you love in need of comfort?
Close your eyes and ask God to be very near to you or

your loved one, providing comfort and love, like a mother with her child in the darkness of the night.

15. The easy yoke

So often I prayed, *God, I am so weary and burdened. Give me rest...give me rest.*

After all, He said, "Come to me, all you who are weary and burdened, and I will give you rest. Take my yoke upon you and learn from me, for I am gentle and humble in heart, and you will find rest for your souls. For my yoke is easy and my burden is light" (Matthew 11: 28-30 NIV).

A yoke is a really challenging metaphor for the Christian life. For yoked oxen to be effective in a field, both animals need to pull in the same direction. If one pulls left, while the other walks straight, it will be an exhausting, frustrating, and often fruitless journey.

I say that I love Jesus.

I say that I want to walk in His ways, and I try to, daily.

And for many years, I willingly said yes to His yoke.

And then I waited. I waited for things to get easier.

But they just got different and harder.

Then I started actively resisting the yoke, pulling away, stalling, and collapsing in exhaustion.

I was constantly shocked at every new hardship, bitterly questioning God's sovereignty, throwing way too many pity parties for myself. I wished I could say, like Paul, "I have learned the secret of being content" (Philippians 4:12 NIV). Sure, at the end of the day, I walked the path with my yoke-partner, but not willingly, not gracefully, joyfully, or contentedly.

When I was a child, I used to think that the yoke and burden Jesus offers was the life of faith: Once we trust Jesus with our lives then everything will be easy, right?

The truth is, life is difficult, overwhelming, and exhausting, and we will have many, many troubles (John

16: 33). My faith has not exempt me from sickness, financial strain, having children with special needs, or mental breakdowns.

But God has gently revealed this truth to my weary heart: Love is the only thing that gives us true rest. It is the opposite of fear (1 John 4:18). The yoke is the security of His presence. It is the way He gently leads us. Love is the easy burden: *Love God, Love Others.*

The path is hard. Life really sucks sometimes.

But His yoke is easy, and His burden is light.

Because in His love, there is honest, deep rest for our weary souls.

Meditation Moment:

Come to me, all you who are weary and burdened, and I will give you rest. Take my yoke upon you and learn from me, for I am gentle and humble in heart, and you will find rest for your souls. For my yoke is easy and my burden is light (Matthew 11: 28-30 NIV)

Are you resisting His yoke? Ask God to help you see, in a new way, how He wants to gently lead you on this unexpected journey.
Ask Him for ways to love Him and the people around you in a deeper way.

16. The waiting place

Have you ever waited days, weeks, or months for *one* phone call (or email)? If you hear a "yes" on the other end of the line, your entire life is going to change. Wild, scary, growing types of change.

My husband and I have been in this situation several times, like when we waited for the phone call that would tell us that he had been accepted for Officer candidacy in the Military, or the time we waited for months to learn whether or not we would be approved to move to England.

So many times, we have looked at each other and said, "I feel like our entire life is on hold."

We were in the Waiting Place.

It's an infuriating place to be.

You feel stuck.

You want to fly out of your skin, but you're forced to stand still.

You want to scream at the sky, the doctor, the therapist, the school, the-powers-that-be, yourself, God: "HURRY UP!!!!"

There are long sleepless nights of "What if...this? What if...that? What if...*nothing*?"

There are long conversations discussing every scenario under the sun and every response to "this one" or "that one" but you can't pick any one because you are in the Waiting Place.

I've been worn out with waiting. I was spent the year we waited for answers from the school about Benji's Special Education Child Study, when we worried about whether or not he would pass first grade, and then again during the months of waiting when we went through our first (2015) and second (2018) Autism diagnosis testing.

Eventually, you come to the end of yourself, like that quiet place you get to when you've cried your eyes out: Your shoulders stop heaving; your breath comes in shaky waves, but it's slowing. And you feel still.

And it's in that still place, when you've run out of scenarios and questions, that you find the Lord waiting to comfort you.

"Be still, and know that I am God," the psalmist writes (Psalm 46:10 NIV).

I've realized that I can't fight my way out of the Waiting Place, like the boy does in *Oh! The Places You'll Go*. It's too exhausting.

But, if I've learned anything in these last few years, it's that waiting doesn't last forever. It (really and truly) does come to an end.

But in the meantime, while my soul is still in the Waiting Place, life goes on. You may feel like life is standing still right now but it isn't.

Your Real Life is happening right now, not three weeks from now, not in nine months, not in the fall, not next year.

For me, even in the Waiting Place, I have work to complete, dinners to cook, stories to read, homework to check, friends to visit, boo-boos to kiss, a husband to dream with, a house to care for.

I have people to love.

Love always moves forward. There is so much Good to be done.

Even in the Waiting Place.

Meditation Moment:
God is our refuge and strength,
A very present help in trouble.
Therefore we will not fear...
Be still and know that I am God (Psalm 46:1-2a; 10a

NIV).

Are you in the Waiting Place right now? Write down the things that are driving you absolutely crazy about waiting.
Then write down the Good Things that you can do right now, even in the middle of waiting.
Make a plan to do one (or more) of those Good Things this week.

17. In the wilderness

Can I just be honest? I love my kids, but I don't really like being a Stay at Home Mom (ACK! did the sky just fall? Am I going to be struck by lightning?).

I crave adult interaction and mental stimulation. I never felt so alive, so watered and fed, as when I was engaged in lively discussion in my classes in Grad School, or when I gave a killer lecture in my own university classroom, or while I mentored young women.

These days, my agenda usually includes the following exciting tasks:

Unloading the dishwasher!

Loading the dishwasher!

Breaking up fights!

Curing The Whiner of whining!

Watching endless episodes of Paw Patrol!

Wearing out the Energizer Bunny so he will—please, for the love!—take a nap this afternoon!

And the laundry…always the laundry…

Those years of grad school and teaching were rich for me; they drenched me with purpose. But this season? It feels a bit like a desert (and not just because we're currently living in Central Texas).

I get up each day, do All the Mom Things, and then fall into bed at night, exhausted.

And then I get up the next day at dark-thirty to do it again.

I feel like I'm spinning my wheels in the sand, always circling back to the beginning, wondering if I am getting anywhere. Then I wonder where I actually *want* to be and what's so wrong with *right here* anyway?

I don't know the answers to these questions.

But I feel like I'm in my own personal wilderness, wandering, looking for the Promised Land.

The wilderness is boring, monotonous, irritating, and long. But it's also a place where the old things die away, making way for new life and growth. At least, that's the truth I'm clinging to by faith.

A few months before we moved from our Familiar-Life-of-fourteen-years-in-Virginia-to- Military-Life, I was thinking about everything I was about to leave behind; I was terrified of the future and (honestly?) a bit resentful that my husband was moving forward with his career and dreams while my career and dreams were slowly drying up.

I was sitting in church one Sunday before our move and we were singing. I don't know what the song was, and I don't know what I was praying in that moment, but I remember that I was struggling with the tension between feeling stuck and the fear of moving forward in this unknown direction.

And God spoke to my soul, in the middle of all my heartache and angst.

He simply said this: *I have not forgotten you.*

There was nothing more. No promises. No vision of what my future would hold. But the truth of those five words brought peace to my anxious heart, calming my soul.

I have not forgotten you. Those five words mean I am known.

I am seen, even the monotony of my everyday #momlife, in doing dishes and laundry on repeat, in every frustrating, halting attempt to try to raise my wild boys to be young men who love God and love people.

My life is boring and monotonous sometimes.

But I'm learning contentment.

I'm learning thankfulness.

I'm learning to dig in where I'm at, to bloom, and perhaps, create an oasis where I am planted.

Because even in the wilderness, I am not forgotten.

And neither are you.

Meditation Moment:
The Lord your God, who is going before you, will fight for you, as he did for you in Egypt, before your very eyes, and in the wilderness. There you saw how the Lord your God carried you, as a father carries his son, all the way you went until you reached this place (Deuteronomy 1: 30-31 NIV).

Are you bored in this season of life? (it's okay to admit it). Do you feel like you are in the wilderness, just spinning your wheels, unsure of where you are going or what the future holds?
Ask God to reassure you of His care and presence today. You are not forgotten.

18. Patience

I used to look at mothers of special needs kids and think, "Wow. I could never do what she does. She has the patience of a saint."

I never stopped to consider how a saint acquired such virtue.

But now, I have kids with special needs and, let me assure you, I am *not* a saint.

Most days, I actively avoid situations that require patience. It's why I made my twins use sippy cups until they were five and why naptime is non-negotiable for my three-year-old. It's why I stern-facedly warn my boys, "DO NOT SPLASH IN THE TUB" before every bath because I just don't have the patience to deal with spilled drinks, whiny children, and tsunamis in the bathrooms.

Then there are the big things, like communication struggles, learning disabilities, sensory meltdowns, and ADHD challenges. A lid, a nap, or a warning won't "fix" these problems. They are complicated, unpredictable, and difficult. They are constant and pervasive. I *know* they are there and yet, they catch me off guard, destroying my attempts at patience at every turn.

For a long time, I operated on the definition that patience is just holding it together until I eventually snap.

And snap I did.

Again and again and again.

I fervently desired the maturity that James talks about: "Consider it pure joy, my brothers and sisters, whenever you face trials of many kinds, because you know that the testing of your faith produces perseverance. Let perseverance finish its work so that you may be mature and complete, not lacking anything"

(James 1:2-4 NIV).

I wanted to be mature and complete, but (honestly?) I didn't want the trials.

I wanted the fruit of patience but I balked against the idea of "long-suffering" (Galatians 5:22-23 KJV).

I constantly felt my own failures, wondering how I could even say "I love you" to my sons, when I constantly fell short of the first definition of true love: "Love is patient" (1st Corinthians 13:4 NIV).

So, I stopped praying for patience (we all know how *that* goes!). I prayed for other things instead:

I prayed that I could understand how my sons' minds worked.

I prayed that my heart would be tender, instead of hard, toward my children.

I prayed that I could love them unconditionally.

And slowly, a new definition of patience formed in my mind: *The willingness to suffer.*

Redefining patience (or really, coming to a true understanding of Biblical patience) has helped me to step away from my own grit-your-teeth patience, and into an others-focused Love for my children.

Because, let's face it, motherhood—and life—is full of suffering, but in many moments, there is a choice: Either I am going to suffer, or I am going to make those around me suffer.

With my son Benji, I've learned that when I lose my cool, he falls apart; he can't listen to me and he just shuts down, sometimes for a long time. Then we are in a worse place, with a huge, angry wedge in our relationship, all over something as silly as a division problem.

In those challenging moments, I'm learning to dig down deep, in the place where prayer resides, breathe to calm my racing heart, and tell myself, *I am willing to suffer in this moment, for the sake of my son, for the sake of our relationship, for the sake of love.*

There is no perseverance without the trial.

There is no Spirit-fruit without suffering.

It is the willingness to suffer that opens the gateway to that saint-like patience I so desire.

And it's worth it, because relationship is my goal, and Love is the foundation, the means, and the prize.

Meditation Moment:

Consider it pure joy, my brothers and sisters, whenever you face trials of many kinds, because you know that the testing of your faith produces perseverance. Let perseverance finish its work so that you may be mature and complete, not lacking anything (James 1:2-4 NIV).

We all have difficult people in our lives that we are trying to love. Who comes to your mind? Spend some time thinking about ways that you could be "willing to suffer" in this relationship to create room for godly love to grow, both in your life and in the life of the person who requires a lot of patience.

19. Rest

"Looks like your vitamin D is a bit low," the doctor said at my follow up appointment. "But other than that, your bloodwork came back normal."

That's it?! There's nothing else wrong with me? I picked up a small bottle of vitamins on the way home but was incredulous that they would cure my bone-deep exhaustion.

But while the doctor's appointments and vitamins didn't "cure" me per se, they did set me on a path of self-reflection. Something in my life needed to change.

In early 2016, I had four children, including a toddler and a nursing baby.

I hadn't slept through the night in nearly three years.

I was teaching online, grading piles of papers every month.

I was blogging twice a week.

I was taking my son to therapy four times a week.

I was volunteering with an organization I loved.

I was mentoring young women.

Oh, and I had a husband too (Kind of forgot about him…whoopsie!).

No wonder you're exhausted, lady! Your life is crazy! I told myself.

I felt God nudging at my soul, calling me to pull back, calling me to rest.

I resisted.

Busy was what I did best. People called me Superwoman and, though I always laughed and brushed away their compliments, deep down I liked being known as someone who could "do it all."

I hated rest. In fact, I was bad at it. I got antsy when I sat still, feeling guilty that I wasn't "doing something." There was always, *always* something to do. And wasn't I doing all the good things that God had brought into my life? Wasn't I trying to do all this for His glory?

But I was breaking under the load. In fact, my body was shutting down.

I was dropping the balls I was juggling—I started forgetting appointments, even when I had them written down in my planner. I was anxious and quick-tempered all of the time. I was falling apart physically, mentally and emotionally when my family needed me to be healthy and whole, or at least on the road to healthy and whole.

Something needed to change.

Finally, after resisting His prompting for months, I turned in my resignation for my job and told the director of the organization I was volunteering for that I needed to step back.

These were needed yet heartbreaking decisions, ones that had deep and long-lasting ramifications for me emotionally and spiritually, but I knew God was calling me to step back from busy and rest.

I love the story of Elijah in 1 Kings: Elijah, through the Lord's fiery power, had just defeated the prophets of Baal, but immediately after this triumph, he was exhausted and fearful for his life after he heard that the queen wanted to kill him. He ran into the wilderness and was so physically, emotionally, and spiritually weary that he wanted to die.

God saw him in his pain and fatigue and did a remarkable thing: He let the poor man sleep. Then He fed him via angel chefs. Then Elijah lay down and slept again. Then the angels fed him again.

God had more in store for Elijah, more plans, more ministry for him to do. But first, Elijah needed to sleep. He needed to eat. He needed to step away from his crazy, busy life and rest.

I don't think resting was Elijah's plan. But it certainly was God's. Because it was only after Elijah rested that God told him what his next step was.

Are you exhausted in this season of your life? Maybe God is calling you to rest. It's okay, really. After all, when we rest, we are following His example (Genesis 2:2).

Sleep. Eat. Take care of yourself.

Rest in his care. Rest some more.

Then wait for Him to tell you what your next step will be.

Meditation Moment:

There remains, then, a Sabbath-rest for the people of God; for anyone who enters God's rest also rests from their works, just as God did from his. Let us, therefore, make every effort to enter that rest, so that no one will perish by following their example of disobedience (Hebrews 4:9-11 NIV).

It's okay to take a break. It's okay to rest. Right now, make a plan for how you are going to integrate rest into your day today, even if it's only for 10-15 minutes.

20. Daily bread

If you were raised in the church or participated in any youth group or faith-based summer camp, you've probably been told that your faith needs to be "loud," in an "on fire" and "change the world" kind of way. These catch-phrases have become our faith-mantras, our daily bread. Anything else seems too boring to really radiate authentic faith.

But, in reality, much of the time God is giving us a slice of whole wheat. And, though we swear that we are wiser than the Israelites, we grumble at the whole wheat, just as they grumbled at their manna. We long for more (like a unicorn cupcake with rainbow sprinkles!), pushing away the good, nourishing, boring whole wheat like a picky toddler.

For me, I want the speaking engagements and the book deals, the adoring students and mentoring relationships, the blog stats and bylines. That's my unicorn cupcake with rainbow sprinkles, all blessed in Jesus' name, of course.

But my daily bread right now is settling sibling squabbles and teaching long division, wiping bottoms and making daily dinners (and breakfast, lunch, and snacks). It's apologizing when I'm harsh to my children, supporting my husband in this (insane) Military Life, praying for the needs of friends in my Facebook feed, and making the occasional dinner for a family after a surgery or new baby.

Some days my faith looks like getting out of bed in the morning, pushing through my anxiety and depression and do All The Things all over again.

Good, nourishing, boring whole wheat bread.

Sometimes faith is simply believing that God is still shaping me in the moments of my Small Life, remembering that even if I long to live large, He has not forgotten me. I long for the whirlwind, but sometimes He's in the whisper—the Still Small Voice (1 Kings 19:11-12).

"Give us this day our daily bread"…and help me to be thankful.

Meditation Moment:
Our Father in heaven,
hallowed be your name,
your kingdom come,
your will be done,
on earth as it is in heaven.
Give us today our daily bread.
And forgive us our debts,
As we also have forgiven our debtors.
And lead us not into temptation,
But deliver us from the evil one (Matthew 6: 9-13 NIV).

What is your Daily Bread? Are you struggling with a picky heart, always longing for more than what you've been given in this season of life? Ask God to help you learn to eat your daily bread with a thankful heart, trusting His provision for the journey He has prepared for you.

21. Incarnational love

I once heard an Autistic man describe Autism as being in a foreign country where you don't understand the language of the natives and no one understands your language. The people you live with want you, love you, and would do anything for you but their depth of the love doesn't change the fact that you just don't speak the same language and you struggle—constantly—to communicate.

What an eye-opening metaphor.

I am not Autistic.

I do not have ADHD.

I do not have learning disabilities.

I am not my children.

So often, we feel like foreigners to each other, struggling to understand each other's language, desires and values. Many times, my frustration gets the better of me, but I'm learning to ask better questions.

Just the other morning I asked one of my sons to get cups for everyone for breakfast. I already had coffee in a mug so when I saw him reach into the cabinet to get a cup for me, I said, "I don't need one. I already have my coffee."

But he still got the cup out and set it down by my place.

My patience level goes up as the level of my coffee goes down and at this moment, my coffee mug was full.

"Did you not hear me?! I don't need a cup!"

My tone did not match this simple scenario, but I was irritated because this was not the first time this had happened. It was more like the thousandth time that I had made a request and he did the exact opposite.

I know he can hear me. I thought. *The pediatrician and the audiologist tested it so I know HE CAN HEAR.*

But when I paused to examine my response and my frustration, I wondered if this wasn't about hearing. What if it was about listening and understanding?

So, I asked him, "When I told you I didn't need a cup, did you think I'll just get her one anyway, or did it just take you a while to process what I said?"

"The second one," he said.

And suddenly another piece clicked into place, one tiny portion of the mosaic that shows me the image of my son. The cup incident showed me, in a greater way, how ADHD affects the way he processes language. It's frustrating for me at times, but more for him.

We are foreigners living in the same home together, struggling to speak the same language, to understand each other's minds.

I remember how Jesus became human, a tiny baby born to human parents, just so he could grow up human, to live in our skin, to speak with a human tongue, to feel our emotions, our joys, our sorrows. What incredible, incomprehensive love: God put on our flesh so that He would no longer be a foreigner to us.

I'm praying that I may have this kind of love for my sons, incarnational love—the ability to somehow enter into their experience, roll around in their minds and hearts, and understand who they are in visceral way.

I know that I will never know what it is truly like to be Autistic or ADHD.

But I'm working on learning their language, even if I'm terrible at it. Each book and article I read, each question I ask, each apology, each pause brings us closer to understanding each other's hearts and minds.

Meditation Moment:

The Word became flesh and made his dwelling among us. We have seen his glory, the glory of the one and only Son, who came from the Father, full of grace and truth…Out of his fullness we have all received grace in place of grace already given (John 1:14; 16 NIV).

Do you need incarnational love for someone in your life? Ask God to help you to see and love this person in a new way.

22. Maybe we aren't meant to move mountains

In 2015, I remember going into the Autism diagnosis process feeling overwhelmed, thinking, *Something needs to change.*

I was ready for that change, to tackle our issues, to overcome our challenges, to move mountains. I had the vague notion when we started all the appointments and therapy, and while I was reading all the books, that we would be able to scale Benji's mountains and overcome his struggles. One step at a time, together, we would climb, conquer, and come out on the other side. But in these crazy, unexpected, growing years since his diagnosis, I'm learning that some mountains don't move.

I've spent a massive amount of mental energy (and personal guilt) trying to discover the causes of Autism. My research and personal experience has led me to this: The causes of Autism are unknown. It is most likely genetic.

In dark, vulnerable moments, my husband and I have asked each other, "Do you wish Benji wasn't Autistic?"

And the answer is always "No." We love our son. We love who he is, his personality, his quirks, his special interests. Being Autistic is who he is, with all its gifts and challenges.

And it is challenging. I've needed a lot of help and support to parent him through the years, from therapy (for him and myself), books, friends who have special need children, and much, much prayer.

In the years since his diagnosis, he has grown so much. We all have. We've gotten stronger, smarter, wiser, braver.

We've overcome many obstacles with the right tools and resources. But some challenges we continue to live with. Some challenges he is going to have to live with for his whole life.

That's what the therapy has been good for—learning to live with these challenges. And when I say, "live with" I don't mean in a just-sigh-and-give-up sort of way. I mean, "live with" in a way that creates Life.

I'm not just focused on overcoming his struggles anymore. I'm working on knowing, understanding, caring for, loving my son, and accepting him for who he is. I'm not trying to move the mountains anymore because I've had to accept this truth: They aren't going to move.

Jesus said, "If you have faith as small as a mustard seed, you can say to this mountain, 'Move from here to there,' and it will move" (Matthew 17:20 NIV). I have faith, small as it may be, but I don't think God is asking me to move these mountains. I think He's asking me to love and live right where I am, where our family is, where Benji is.

So, I'm trying. Day by day, moment by moment.

I'm learning to live in the life He has given me.

I'm learning to make our home in the mountains.

Meditation Moment:
I know what it is to be in need, and I know what it is to have plenty. I have learned the secret of being content in any and every situation, whether well fed or hungry, whether living in plenty or in want. I can do all this through him who gives me strength (Philippians 4:12-13 NIV).

Contemplate ways you can make yourself at home in your life today. Do you need to hug someone, read a book you've been avoiding, make an important phone call, hang pictures, give away clothes that don't fit, or let go of long-held dream?

Ask God to help you learn to be content where you are today.

23. Real life

We had been married for eight months when I saw two lines on the test. I was twenty-two and finishing my last semester of college. We always wanted to have kids, but not *now*. The life we had carefully planned and dreamed about slipped through our fingers like sand.

When we found out we were having twins, our friends said, "Woah," their eyes and mouths perfect circles of shock and awe.

"I know," we said, our souls mimicking their reactions.

We felt like our life was over.

We wanted all the highs that we thought being an adult would bring: Diplomas, celebrations, promotions, travel, vacations, independence, and big toys. We wanted to taste the adult life we had always craved.

I quickly added up the years in my head. *Forty-one.* We would be forty-one when they graduated from high school. *Then* we would get our life back.

Over ten years have passed since then and now, looking back, I am ashamed of my attitude, how I wanted to wish the years away until we somehow got back to "real life."

But do you know what?

Real Life happened.

It just took us a few years to recognize it.

God, in His wisdom, plucked us away from our pristine blueprints, planted us in a 1950s fixer-upper with two wild baby boys and said, "Grow."

We were promoted to "Mommy and Daddy," a sacred honor and jaw-dropping responsibility. We celebrated when babies finally slept through the night, when our twins recovered from their tonsillectomies, and later when our 2nd grader became part of the 100 Point Reading Club at school.

We now appreciate the luxury of travel without kids and know the true price of independence.

Forget about Big Toys. We wonder why we have so much crap in our basement.

Oh, and we didn't need to worry about the diplomas. Between the two of us, we've earned five degrees since we found out we were pregnant in 2007.

I spent a long time mourning the life I thought I was going to have and wishing away the years until my Real Life would start.

But the Real is all around me:

Real flesh and blood children, full of warmth and silky hair, sticky kisses and heavy heads on my shoulder.

Real bills and grocery shopping and home improvement projects and problem solving as a couple.

Real smiles and inside jokes and farting kids and laughing until we cry.

Real fights and shouting and apologizing and relationship building.

Real conversations about God and our dreams, both old and shifted, and how they overlap.

This is the stuff that makes up Real Life.

I wish I could go back to my 22-year-old self and tell that scared girl who was about to become a mom, "It isn't going to look like you planned. *You* aren't going to look like you planned. But don't wish it away, because your Real Life *is* happening right now."

Meditation Moment:

This is what the Lord says: "When seventy years are completed for Babylon, I will come to you and fulfill my good promise to bring you back to this place. For I know the plans I have for you," declares the Lord, "plans to prosper you and not to harm you, plans to give you hope and a future. Then you will call on me and come and pray to me, and I will listen to you. You will seek me and find me when you seek me with all your heart (Jeremiah 29: 10-13 NIV).

Does your Real Life look different than you thought it would? Spend a few moments laughing, crying or both about how life has turned out differently than you expected.

24. Cultivating faithfulness

The movers were scheduled. I was days away from moving to Kansas to be with my parents while my husband traveled to Oregon for a month of training before we moved to England for our dream military assignment. But that's when all our plans came crashing down.

Due to a misunderstanding in our medical paperwork, we were "not recommended for travel." In non-military speak, that meant "You've been denied. You're out."

Not only did we suffer a huge change in our plans and a heart-crushing disappointment, we also had to find a new place to live because our landlords had already leased our home to new tenants. Three days later, I found myself in a 900 square foot apartment (half our household goods were now in a storage unit) wondering what had just happened to my life.

We couldn't go back.

We couldn't move forward.

All I could do was wait for other people to make decisions about my life.

And I hated it.

I'm a planner by nature. If I go to the grocery store without a list, I'm in "wild woman" mode. I love knowing what I'm doing for the day, the week, the semester, next year.

But during this season of infuriating, paralyzing waiting, I couldn't plan anything. Not where I was going to live, not activities for the kids (should we sign up for soccer? Probably not, we may be moving in a few weeks), not my own personal goals, like looking for editing jobs—with our plans so uncertain, how could I commit to projects right now?

God, what am I supposed to do? I prayed in frustration. *How am I supposed to live?*

And He brought a word to mind: *Faithfulness.*

Live faithfully, He whispered to my soul. *Right here, right now. Serve well where you are. Love well where you are. Today.*

I wanted to laugh. It was so easy.

I wanted to cry. It was so hard.

But I tried.

When I found myself cursing the tiny kitchen with the drawers that fell out every time I opened them, and the faulty dishwasher that only cleaned the dishes half the time, I reminded myself to be thankful that we had a place to live and food to feed our children.

When I longed for work outside of my home, I pulled myself back to the present where homeschooling and raising four wild boys needed my full focus.

When I wanted to scroll for hours through potential houses in England (where we may or may not live), I forced myself to shut my laptop and say, "Not right now."

When I was in tears, wondering "why is this happening to us?" my husband reminded me of who had opened the doors to the military life in the first place.

Faithfulness.

Faithfulness to the path we were on.

Faithfulness to love the people I was with.

Faithfulness in the here and now when I couldn't dream about the future.

Faithfulness even when I didn't like where I was at, when I was disappointed, bored, and ached for change.

It's a hard, transformative daily choice to live in the present, to accept my circumstances, to choose to love well where I am.

But I know that in choosing faithfulness, I am in good company. Jesus, the most beautiful example of faithfulness, is with me every step of the way.

Meditation Moment:
Teach me your way, Lord,
    that I may rely on your faithfulness;
give me an undivided heart,
    that I may fear your name (Psalm 86:11 NIV).

What about you? Is God calling you to dig deeper instead of wider? Is He calling you to stay put when you want to go? Today, in the middle of your ordinary, boring life, how can you cultivate faithfulness?

25. Changed for good

The realization came swiftly as I glanced at the calendar on the side of my fridge while in the middle of feeding my four boys breakfast: August 24. It was my due date for the baby we lost to miscarriage: *Izzy.* You never forget your due date, do you?

In previous years, this day brought tears and mourning, even tangible depression in the days leading up to the due date. But this year, I felt contemplative, my mind circling back, remembering all the days and all the ways my miscarriage changed my life.

Grief has a way of rearranging your soul, like a tornado sweeping through and leaving you stunned, sitting among the emotional wreckage of your life, asking yourself, "Where do I go from here?"

I don't know if grief is like this for everyone; every person is different. But because I joined this Club (the one no one wants to join), I've developed more acute listening skills and the new-found ability to weep with those who weep.

But I didn't always say the right thing, like the one time I told a new friend who told me about her miscarriage, "Well, I'm sure you'll get pregnant again soon."

She looked at me with wise, sad eyes. "I have no guarantee."

And it was true. Her miscarriage was many years ago and she was never able to get pregnant again.

I felt ashamed at my assumptions, but through that conversation I learned that sometimes it is better to just listen or say, "I'm so sorry. That's really hard," rather than rely on clichés to give shallow comfort.

My miscarriage also gave me the gift of greater compassion for women who are suffering, and not just for those who have lost a baby. My eyes were opened to the suffering of women who experience infertility as well. I had no idea the heartbreaking difficulty many women go through on their journey to become mothers. Although I couldn't empathize with their pain, my own loss enlarged my ability to sympathize with women who are going through this private agony.

Before my miscarriage, I had never written so openly about my inner life before, but the support and comfort I received as a result was life changing. So many women wrote me private messages and emails, telling me their stories and letting me know that reading my story brought them comfort.

Later, the bravery birthed by writing about my miscarriage helped me to write about my son's learning disabilities, his Autism diagnosis, ADHD, and my struggles to adjust my expectations about motherhood, which now looked so radically different than what I thought my life would look like.

And then?

The *Mothering Beyond Expectations Collective Blog* was born. Since October 2016, by collecting and sharing stories of women who are mothering beyond their own expectations, this website has been viewed nearly 100,000 times from readers around the world. I am so humbled and honored to share these stories every week, to see people respond, to hear them say "me too" and realize they are not alone in their struggles.

It is a gift that brings me great joy and purpose.

And yet…

Sometimes I think, *If I could trade it all to have my baby in my arms, would I?*

I don't know.

I don't know.

As humans we are constantly evaluating, trying to pinpoint the Life Changing Events, the ones that we stop and say, "You know, if this had never happened…"

My miscarriage was one of those Life Changing Events.

When I looked around my table on August 24th, I felt the ache of my missing child, the one I will never know on this side of heaven. Yet I know that if Izzy had been born, Eli would not be here.

It's complicated.

It's confusing.

It was never what I expected.

I was only Izzy's mom for a few short weeks but her presence brought me so much joy and hope during that time. She is gone now, but by sharing my story, and all the other stories that were born out of my heartbreak, my hope is that I can bring joy and hope to others.

Have I been changed for the better?

I don't know.

But I do know that I have been changed for good.

Meditation Moment:
"Blessed are those who mourn, for they will be comforted" (Matthew 5:4 NIV).

Have you been changed for good by grief? Take a few moments to reflect on some of the Life Changing Events in your life. Ask God to help you see the outcome of those events from His perspective.

26. Talents

Growing up, I remember hearing numerous sermons preached on the "Parable of the Talents" from Matthew 25 (NKJV). In the parable, Jesus challenged His listeners to consider how they are using the "talents" the master has given them: Are you investing two fold, five fold, ten fold? Or are you the wicked servant who buries his master's money in the ground?

In Jr. high and high school, I remember fervently praying, searching my soul and heart's desires: What were MY talents? Was I using what God had given me?

Many of my youth pastors and summer camp speakers transliterated "talent" (a sum of money) to the modern day English version of "talent": a gifting, or natural ability. Clever, right? Well, sort of. In my adolescent mind, I reduced the meaning of this parable neatly into the definition of "how am I using my giftings or natural abilities in the church?"

As a teen, I eagerly identified my talents as musical so I played the piano for the offering and sang specials during the Sunday service. In college, I used my leadership abilities to become a prayer leader in my dorm. As an adult, I have used my creative writing skills to support a friend's vision to create graphic novels to provide education and support to those at risk for Human Trafficking in the United States.

But as I've journeyed farther in my Christian walk, as I've experienced more heartache, more questions, more unexpected obstacles, some new thoughts have developed in my mind: What do I do with the other "talents" I've been given, the confusing, painful, difficult circumstances?

Can God use the intense pain and suffering found in this life, like eating disorders; unplanned pregnancy;

bankruptcy; divorce; boring, monotonous work; a devastating car accident; chronic health problems; the death of a loved one; estrangement from family members; miscarriage (and so much more) for His glory?

So often, my response to the pain and suffering in my life is to complain about it, wish my circumstances were different, or "bury it" in the ground, trying to forget it ever happened, echoing the servant in the parable who says "I was afraid, and went and hid your talent in the ground. Look, there you have what is yours" (Matthew 25:25 NKJV).

But God has shown me that, if I ask Him, He will show me how He can use anything to serve Him because He is actively seeking to redeem our suffering and pain. He longs to unearth what we have buried and show us new ways of living in His Kingdom.

May we seek to invest in life, hope, and redemption, actively working to return two, five and tenfold to our Master when He comes, our ears longing for these words: "Well done, good and faithful servant; you have been faithful over a few things, I will make you ruler over many things. Enter into the joy of your lord" (Matthew 25:23 NKJV).

Meditation Moment:
Give, and it will be given to you. A good measure, pressed down, shaken together and running over, will be poured into your lap. For with the measure you use, it will be measured to you (Luke 6:38 NIV).

Are you "burying" the uncomfortable parts of your life in the ground, the parts that are painful and messy? Ask God to reveal the ways He longs to redeem the difficult and painful situations in your life for His glory.

27. Hope and healing

I was in the waiting room at the ear doctor, waiting with ten-month-old Eli. An elderly woman smiled at us and asked, "Is he your first?"

I laughed and said, "He's my fourth—my fourth boy!"

She smiled, "I bet he has fun with his brothers!"

I agreed and we admired my baby together for a few moments.

Then she offered, "I have a boy and a girl."

I nodded. "Are they close in age?"

Her smile quickly faded and a sudden pain crossed her face. "No…they are eight years apart."

Just then, the nurse called us back. But as I stood up, the woman said quietly, "I had a lot of trouble."

I wish I could have asked her to tell her story but our time together ended as quickly as it began.

Maybe she hoped and prayed for a baby for eight years after her firstborn.

Maybe she only has two babies on this side of heaven.

Her grief, probably fifty-plus years old, rose easily to the surface, raw and real.

Her motherhood story did not look like she thought it would.

And I realized something, something heavy and heartbreaking: Some wounds, without the right support, do not—cannot—heal.

So, what do we do, when we meet a stranger, or a friend, or a family member (or even ourselves), and the pain of their reality overturns the picture of what they thought their life would look like?

How do we face our expectations in order to heal and keep moving forward?

I think the first step, often, is acknowledging that our pain is real. Sometimes we think that being strong means saying, "I'm fine. It's no big deal."

We hide, we stuff, we shrug, we dismiss.

But then we hear another person's story, and it reminds us of that tucked away place in our hearts, the place that still aches when bumped unexpectedly.

I wish I could have heard her story. I would have been honored to share the weight of her grief for a small moment, to acknowledge her pain as real, to assure her that her story, as unexpected as it might have been, was meaningful.

There is so much power in sharing our stories, and in turn, listening to the stories of others. It is hard to heal when our pain is tucked away, buried under years and the lies that "no one wants to hear about that hard time I went through." Sometimes a moment—a "Me too"—is enough to let healing begin. By sharing and listening, we can help to bear the weight of pain, if only for a moment.

I only caught a glimpse of the story of the mother I met in the waiting room. There was so much weight in her words: "I had a lot of trouble."

We all have trouble: that's a universal truth of what it means to be human.

But we don't have to shoulder our struggles alone.

Let's share our stories.

Let's listen.

Let's bear one another's burdens.

Together, with God's grace, we can find hope and healing.

Meditation Moment:
Praise be to the God and Father of our Lord Jesus Christ, the Father of compassion and the God of all comfort, who comforts us in all our troubles, so that we can comfort those in any trouble with the comfort we

ourselves receive from God (2 Corinthians 1:3-4 NIV).

List the most difficult experiences you have gone through in your life. Did you receive comfort from others? How do you wish you would have been comforted?
Write down some ways you could comfort others in the future who have gone through similar situations as you.

28. When God provides

It's scary how doubt creeps up behind you and latches onto your soul, like a dark, silent parasite, draining away your faith.

Is God there?

Does anyone hear me?

What is the point of praying?

Prayer is as familiar to me as breathing, but doubt is well-known to me too, especially when it comes to the gritty prayers for tangible needs. Like, if God knows that, deep in my heart, I think He isn't going to come through, is the prayer pointless? If my faith is smaller than a mustard seed, is it even worth planting?

Right after Aaron left for officer school, I had a gutter company come to the house to give me an estimate to replace our soffits, facias and gutters, an essential job that needed to be done before we put our house on the market. The work was going to take a chunk out of our meager bank account but we thought we could make it work.

But when the gutter guy gave me the estimate of $3000, I smiled, thanked him, and then went to my room and cried. We thought the work would be around $1200-$1500. There was no way we could afford $3000. It was impossible.

I cried and prayed, "Lord, please provide for our needs," all the while wondering, *How?*

Then I remembered that we had talked about asking my brother for a loan if we got in a pinch. I hoped the pinch would never come but here it was, painfully squeezing out all other options. So, I took a deep, shaky breath and talked to my brother that morning. He immediately and graciously offered to loan us the money.

I was so thankful, but it was a huge kick in the gut. I felt so low, having to ask others for money to fix our house.

The work was delayed on the gutters because of massive rain. Finally, they started the work—but then more rain. The foreman said he would finish on a Tuesday, but then, in an act of generosity, he worked all day on Sunday so his men could finish up on Monday.

On the Friday before they finished the work though, I was invited to a lovely, going-away party with some ladies from our church. They poured encouragement into me, and we all ate good food and laughed and had wonderful conversation.

As the party was wrapping up, a dear friend—a woman who is widowed and retired—pulled me aside and asked, "Can I ask you something? Can I send you a check?"

My immediate response was to refuse—it was on the tip of my tongue to say, "Oh, no! You don't have to do that!" But her face looked so hopeful that I found myself saying, "Yes, you may. I won't say no."

Her face lit up. "Oh good! I already looked up your address."

She was beyond delighted, her reaction soothing my complicated feelings.

So, two days later, on Monday, the men finished the gutter work. My brother sent the money to my bank account. Everything seemed in place. I thanked him profusely but I wondered, with a sigh, how long it would take us to pay him back.

Then on Monday afternoon, I checked the mailbox and found a small card.

It was from my widowed, retired friend.

I smiled at her lovely cursive note: *Dearest Brittany, You are going through a challenging time. It may be hard to believe, but the day will come when you will look back and it will seem like a short time. I've had wearing times which seemed to stretch on and on and I couldn't see the end, but the end of these times did come. God resolves one problem at a time, and I know your great faith will be rewarded. As for the enclosed check, don't think it's a big thing...I can do without this without any problem.*

I finished her note, and unfolded the check, expecting a generous gift of $100 or even $200. But my mouth fell open as something like a holy presence rushed into my kitchen.

The check was for $3000.

It was the very amount I needed on the very day the gutters were finished. I could now pay my brother back immediately.

I was astonished. It was a jaw-dropping, overflowing, right-on-time answer to my prayer, prayed in tears one month ago. And yet I wanted to laugh at my pitiful faith, because I prayed for God to provide and then I was surprised when He did.

Maybe that makes God laugh too, in a good-natured way: *See? I'm here. I hear you. I know your needs. I'm going to take care of you.*

That mustard seed of faith grew, even though it was buried under a heap of doubt. But my faith is growing; it's stronger than ever because God hears us. He loves us and His provision is greater than our weakest prayers.

Meditation Moment:
And my God shall supply all your need according to His riches in glory by Christ Jesus. Now to our God and Father be glory forever and ever. Amen (Philippians 4:19-20 NKJV).

Are you in great need right now, financially or otherwise? Ask God to provide. He hears you. He loves you. He is a good Father who loves to give good gifts to His children (Matthew 7:11).

Take some time to reflect on how God has provided for your needs in the past. He is able to do it again. Trust His heart, His goodness, and His timing.

29. Celebration

When my third son, Silas, was born in October of 2012, I felt like I had finally hit my groove in motherhood. My twins were five and had amazing teachers in pre-K. I loved being home with my new baby and teaching part time at a local university and online. Life was good.

I am so happy, I remember thinking.

But we've had some hard times since that Happy Year.

Fourteen months later, I had a miscarriage.

Benji started struggling in first grade.

I had another baby boy and his babyhood was not easy like it was with Silas.

I fought with our local elementary school about doing a child study to discover if Benji had learning disabilities (He did).

Then Benji was diagnosed with Autism, and he and Micah were both diagnosed as ADHD.

Due to all this stress, I quit teaching, which created its own brand of melancholy.

My husband joined the Military and we ended up living in three different homes in twelve months.

I was in Survival Mode. Sometimes I feel like I'm still there, like I'm still trying to recover from the wind being knocked out of me. Life's giant curve balls *hurt*. But going beyond Survival Mode takes a lot of effort, especially if you've been in survival mode for a long time and your life has lots of stress and lots of complications.

Strength, I found myself praying, exhausted by babies who *still* did not sleep through the night and endless appointments with teachers, doctors, and therapists. *Please give me strength.*

A verse from childhood came to mind: "The joy of the Lord is your strength" (Nehemiah 8:10 NIV).

But what does that mean anyway? Growing up, I thought it meant "put-on-a-happy-face-grin-and-bear-it," but I am so beyond manufactured, plastic-Christianity at this point in my life.

But when I prayed for strength, God told me to celebrate.

At first, this seemed like a weird answer to my prayer, because putting the effort into anything "extra" in my life is exhausting.

But I decided to try it, try out-of-the-ordinary celebrating.

When Micah and Benji made honor roll at school we went outside our normal "I'm-so-proud-of-you's" and indulged in a "formal" celebration by getting a babysitter for the two little boys and taking the twins out to dinner at Buffalo Wild Wings. Then we went to a trampoline park for thirty minutes of bouncing and hilarity.

We had a wonderful time, so good that it surprised me. We had good food, good conversation, sincere smiles, and genuine laughter. I felt shocked when I realized that this was the first time since our younger two boys were born that we had taken our twins out for special time with mom and dad.

The joy of those hours pushed away the fog that comes from the monotony of Everyday Life and gave me an unexpected peace. And with that peace came strength too, strength that said, "You're doing okay. You have good kids. Look—your kids are strong and healthy and smiling. Sure, you're kinda messed up but overall, you have a happy family."

We celebrated and we rose above Survival Mode for a few hours.

We don't have the money to do restaurants and trampoline parks on a regular basis but I've been looking for small ways to celebrate in our everyday life.

One night, I lit a candle at the dinner table.

"What's that for?" My husband asked.

"Just for fun," I replied.

Just for fun: A small moment of effort, a spark of beauty in the middle of the mundane moments of everyday life.

Just for joy.

My life is challenging, but I'm trying to dig my way out of Survival Mode, one small moment of celebration at a time. It's the out-of-the-ordinary, created moments of joy that are giving me strength these days.

When we delight in the life that that's been created for us by God, we find the strength to keep on living it, day by day, moment by moment, joy by joy.

Meditation Moment:
Though the fig tree does not bud
   and there are no grapes on the vines,
though the olive crop fails
   and the fields produce no food,
though there are no sheep in the pen
   and no cattle in the stalls,
yet I will rejoice in the Lord,
   I will be joyful in God my Savior (Habakkuk 3:17-18 NIV).

Are you in Survival Mode right now? What is one way you can celebrate or create a moment of fun or joy today or this week?

30. Carry each other's burdens

My motherhood journey has looked wildly different than I thought it would be.

On many occasions, I have literally thrown up my hands, saying, "I've got nothing. I have no idea what to do." All I can do is ride the wave of that moment, or day, or month, and pray we all come out intact on the other side.

Sometimes I've stood on the edge of that deep, black pit of the unknown, wondering if I am going to fall in. Other times, it's only when I look back, far removed from the experience, that I realize how close I was to giving up.

I've written about many of these dark times on my blog and, when I look back at my posts, I know I probably overshare in my writing—it was one of my faults when I taught in the classroom too. When the semester ended, all my students knew way more about me (and my husband, kids, and first crush) than I did about them.

But sometimes I think that if I *didn't* share (blogging or otherwise) I'd step over the edge, into all that blackness, and tumble down, down, down.

But it's not just the act of blogging or the story-telling, though that's cathartic.

It's the sharing.

It's a way of saying, "I have a burden. Will you help me carry it?"

We all need a good friend to listen to us vent about our bad days. The sharing helps us unload the burden. In those really dark moments, it helps us back away from the edge.

But sharing is a two-way street. Every good friend knows that you can't just vent about your own bad day—you have to make space to listen too. And, for me, this act of "making space" has been key to me not succumbing to the despair of my depression in some of my darkest moments.

I love this quote by Rachel Macy Stafford, blogger at *Hands Free Mama*, in her blog post, "Your Role in a Loved One's Struggle": "On the other side of despair is connection—connection that comes from recognizing a familiar look of pain in someone else's eyes and reaching out your hand."

The greatest gift I have been given as a result of sharing the stories that make up my life is that on a regular basis, I have friends (and even strangers!) send me private messages saying, "me too." They share their stories with me, stories of their grief, their waiting, their adjustment of their expectations, and always their overwhelming love for their family and friends.

I share. They share. We carry each other's burdens. We back away from the edge, hand in hand, walking towards light with renewed hope, together.

Everybody has something, but you aren't alone in your pain.

Take the first step—share your story.

You never know how God will use this unexpected season to bring hope to another person.

Meditation moment:
Carry each other's burdens, and in this way you will fulfill the law of Christ (Galatians 2:6 NIV).

You have a story to share. Whose burden could you help lighten today by sharing your story, even if it is just with one person?
Is there an email, message, text, or phone call you could make that could encourage someone today?

31. You are the light of the world

This little light of mine
I'm gonna let it shine.

Did you, like me, sing out those words, holding up your finger in the air, shouting "Hide it under a bushel? No! I'm gonna let it shine!" for everyone in the world (or at least at Vacation Bible School) to hear?

Such an easy, joyful song to sing.

It's a lot more complicated to live out. How do we let our light shine?

What if we don't even know what our light is?

Jesus said that a city on a hill, like a light on a lampstand, cannot be hidden (Matthew 5:14-15). When I think, *What is my light?* I need to consider the things in my life that cannot be concealed from others, but even deeper, from myself.

What are the things in my life that consume my waking moments, that I love to talk about, or that are constantly on my mind? The fact that I'm a mom of four, crazy, amazing boys; my boys' special needs; our military-life adventures; social justice issues that I am passionate about; great books I've read; my depression and anxiety; anything Jane Austen (because once upon a time, I wrote my Master's Thesis about her works); a dinner recipe my kids actually ate without complaining; my body-image insecurities; where we are going to live next month (or in the next 3 years); my latest parenting screw-up with my kids.

These are the things that fill my mind and days, the things that cannot be hidden (even if I try to forget or stuff them down at times).

Many of these passions, activities, or obsessions don't seem all that special, or even all that spiritual (some of them are even sinful), but as I've walked with

Him, God has shown me that He can use *anything* to make a new and deeper connection to another person, *anything* to spread more love and kindness, *anything* for His glory.

God wants to use the unique make-up of our lives— our personalities, interests, successes, failures, and the deep, dark secrets that fill our minds and waking moments—for His glory.

It's the deep, dark moments of our story that scare us though. Those are the parts that we want to bury, to hide away under the bushel.

Surely God couldn't use that, we think.

But the truth is, God delights in bringing light to dark places. Wasn't His first act, in all of creation, to bring light in the darkness (Genesis 1:3)?

He longs to do the same for you.

He wants to show you how everything that makes you *you*, when viewed through the lens of His redemption, is your light.

This is what you have to offer to the world.

This is what God has given you to help you build connections and relationships with others, to spread love, to bring hope to the hopeless, to bring Him glory.

Don't hide your light under a bushel.

Meditation Moment:
You are the light of the world. A city that is set on a hill cannot be hidden. Nor do they light a lamp and put it under a basket, but on a lampstand, and it gives light to all who are in the house. Let your light so shine before men, that they may see your good works and glorify your Father in heaven (Matthew 5:14-16 NKJV).

What is your light? What is part of your story that would bring you joy to share with someone in your life? Sometimes we know we could share parts of our life with

others but the act of sharing seems too scary right now.
Ask God to work through those fears with you.
Ask Him, also, to reveal new ways to share your light
with others.

Acknowledgements

Many thanks to my dear friends Brett, Debbie, Haley, Laura, Lauren, Sarah, and Savannah who gifted me with their proofreading, editing, and revision skills and advice. I so appreciate each of you for your time, careful eyes for all those little words I left out, and kind, encouraging words.

Thank you, Sabrena, for looking at my terrible cover design drafts and then giving me professional graphic design advice so that I could arrive at a fairly decent cover (for a complete amateur!).

Thank you also, Bethany, for all the beautiful promotional images you made for me!

Thank you, Aaron, for being my partner on our unexpected journey. There is no one else I would rather do life with. You inspire me every day as you live out your dreams and press forward to become a better man than you were the day before. I love you. Thanks for giving me advice and encouragement on this book and for telling me that I have a cute face.

Thank you to everyone on my launch team! I *so* appreciate your willingness to help me promote *Unexpected* and to push this little book into the world.

Thank you to everyone who has told me they are excited for this book and for refraining from saying "You are crazy, lady!" for writing it during this insane season of life as we are in the middle of uprooting our whole family from the USA and hopping over the pond to replant ourselves in England for the next three years.

About the author

Brittany A. Meng is married to Aaron and together they have four boys, Micah, Benji, Silas, and Eli. Home is where the Military sends them. They are currently headed to England so you can follow all their "Pip, pip, cheerio!" adventures (as Silas calls them!) on TheBamBlog.com!

Her writing has been featured on ScaryMommy, The Mighty, Coffee+Crumbs, For Every Mom, Christianity Today: Her.Menutics, Care-Net, BlogHer and SheKnows.

She is the creator and editor of *Mothering Beyond Expectations*, a collective blog that features stories of "grief, grace, and growth for the modern mom." Do you have a story to share? She is always looking for guest writers!

She writes about the grit and grace of her personal life at TheBamBlog.com.

Find her on Facebook at The Bam Blog and Mothering Beyond Expectations Collective Blog. Follow her by email at TheBamBlog.com.

83828748R00061

Made in the USA
Middletown, DE
15 August 2018